STORM CHASER

SUSAN H. GRAY

Published in the United States of America by Cherry Lake Publishing
Ann Arbor, Michigan
www.cherrylakepublishing.com

Content Adviser: Warren Faidley, extreme weather journalist and survival expert
Reading Adviser: Marla Conn, ReadAbility, Inc.

Photo Credits: © Craig ONeal/Flickr Images, cover, 1, 16; © Mr Twister/Shutterstock Images, 5; Courtesy
of U.S. AIR FORCE, 6; © Todd Shoemake/Shutterstock Images, 8; © A. T. Willett/Alamy, 11; Courtesy of U.S. AIR
FORCE, 12; © Melanie Metz/Shutterstock Images, 15; © Ryan McGinnis/Alamy, 17, 21; © Harvepino/Shutterstock
Images, 18; © Martin Haas/Shutterstock.com, 22; #© Tim Pleasant/Thinkstock Images, 24; © Lisa F. Young/
Shutterstock Images, 27; © RON T. ENNIS/KRT/Newscom, 28

Library of Congress Cataloging-in-Publication Data

Gray, Susan H.
  Storm chaser / Susan H. Gray.
    pages cm.—(Cool STEAM careers)
  Includes index.
  ISBN 978-1-63362-565-5 (hardcover)—ISBN 978-1-63362-745-1 (pdf)—ISBN 978-1-63362-655-3 (pbk.)—
ISBN 978-1-63362-835-9 (ebook)
  1. Severe storms—Juvenile literature. 2. Storm chasers—Juvenile literature. I. Title. II. Series: 21st century skills
library. Cool STEAM careers.

  C941.3.G73 2016
  551.55023--dc23
                                    2015005366

Cherry Lake Publishing would like to acknowledge the work of
the Partnership for 21st Century Skills. Please visit www.p21.org
for more information.

Printed in the United States of America
Corporate Graphics

ABOUT THE AUTHOR

Susan H. Gray has a master's degree in zoology and has written many reference books for children
and young adults. In her free time, she enjoys traveling, gardening, and playing the piano. Susan
and her husband, Michael, live in Cabot, Arkansas, with their many pets.

TABLE OF CONTENTS

STEAM is the acronym for Science, Technology, Engineering, Arts, and Mathematics. In this book, you will read about how each of these study areas is connected to a career in storm chasing.

CHAPTER 1

TWISTER!

Kevin and Becca ran toward their dad's car. It was the last day of school, and they were ready to start their summer vacation. "Hurry!" their dad shouted. "They say bad weather is on the way." Kevin hurried into the car, but Becca paused for just a moment. She noticed that the wind was picking up. The sky was a sickly greenish gray. Tornado weather! She quickly hopped into the backseat. Their dad pulled out into traffic and headed toward home.

Driving in a thunderstorm can be difficult and dangerous.

Soon, the wind was howling. Large raindrops were hitting the windshield. As they drove on, they passed a car that had pulled over. Three people were outside the car. One held a large video camera on his shoulder. The other two were unloading equipment from the trunk.

"Who would be out on a day like this?" Kevin asked.

"They're storm chasers, Kev," his dad replied. "They work for the university. Part of their research involves

Meteorologists interpret data from storms.

gathering storm data. They even collect information directly from oncoming tornadoes."

As their dad continued, Becca and Kevin learned more. Most storm chasers are ordinary people fascinated by weather, or **enthusiasts**. They may travel hundreds of miles just to see a storm. They love the adventure, the thrill, and even the danger. For them, storm chasing is a hobby or an extreme sport.

Some storm chasers are members of film crews. They want to capture exciting storm scenes for TV shows, Web sites, and newscasts. Others are photographers. They hope to sell their photos to newspapers or magazines. Still others are people who want to share the thrill of storms with others. They operate storm-chasing tours that allow people to experience the excitement in person.

Professional meteorologists also chase storms. Meteorologists are scientists who study the weather. They try to predict storms so they can warn people to stay out of danger. The weather reporter at your local

THINK ABOUT TECHNOLOGY

Some storm chasers go into the field with video cameras that can capture thousands of images each second. This is perfect for events that occur quickly, such as lightning. Scientists can download the images, watch them in slow motion, or view individual frames. This way, they can see the tiny details of how lightning develops and travels.

Tornadoes can be extremely dangerous.

8

radio or TV station might be a meteorologist. Many meteorologists work for city, state, or national weather centers. Some teach at universities or do research. Usually, storm chasing is a very small part of the work they do.

Storm chasers mostly chase tornadoes. A tornado is a violent storm with a column of air that whirls around in a circle. Observers see it as a dark, funnel-shaped cloud reaching down to the ground. This spinning funnel of air is called a **vortex**. Because of their coiling wind patterns, tornadoes are also called twisters. Wind speeds inside the vortex can exceed 300 miles (483 kilometers) per hour. Such high winds can lift cars and fling them through the air!

CHAPTER 2

A STORMY HISTORY

Storms have fascinated people for centuries, but the practice of chasing them did not exist before 1956. That's when the "father of storm chasing," David Hoadley, began pursuing them in his native North Dakota. Not long after that, he began to follow storms in some of the more tornado-**prone** states.

Another North Dakotan, Roger Jensen, got hooked on storms as a young man. Later, he went on to chase and photograph them. Neil Ward was the first to use his storm-chasing hobby to help meteorologists. While

Joel Ewing and Warren Faidley track a tornado in Kansas.

chasing a 1961 tornado in Oklahoma, he passed on information to the state weather bureau.

Slowly, the community of storm chasers grew. In 1977, Hoadley founded *Storm Track*, the first newsletter for chasers. Within a few years, it had hundreds of readers.

Warren Faidley was the first nonscientist to chase storms as a full-time job. He began his career in the 1980s as a newspaper reporter and photographer. Faidley started the first company that sold photos and videos of severe storms.

A "hurricane hunter" in the U.S. Air Force looks at data as he flies through Hurricane Bill in 2009.

The disaster movie *Twister* came out in 1996. Meteorologists say that the movie is full of scientific errors. Still, this movie and similar TV shows from the early 2000s unleashed a flood of new amateur chasers.

People chase storms all over the world. They may follow **typhoons**, thunderstorms, or hurricanes. But more tornadoes occur in the United States than anywhere else. Most show up in a zone called Tornado Alley, from Texas to North Dakota. Tornadoes can occur at any time of the year. However, in Tornado Alley, the heaviest season is March through June. This is when chasers are out in full force.

THINK ABOUT SCIENCE

Many sciences contribute to the understanding of weather. Physics, for example, can help us understand how lightning behaves. Right now, physicists are trying to understand how lightning develops within a storm and why it travels the pathway it does. Some are also studying why lightning strikes some things on the ground and not others.

CHAPTER 3

STORM CHASERS TODAY

Most storm chasers follow their interest purely as a hobby. In some cases, they take classes from the National Weather Service (NWS) where they learn what to look for in storms and how to stay safe. Hobbyists often shoot photos or videos that they post on the Internet.

Some storm chasers take this to the next level. With training and experience in photography, film, or **videography**, they capture stunning images of weather **phenomena**. They often use high-quality cameras to catch lightning, tornadoes, or hurricanes—or their

Some storm chasers sell their photographs and videos to be used in the news and other places.

aftermath. They sell their photos or videos to television stations, networks, magazines, newspapers, or **stock photo agencies**.

This may sound exciting, but it has drawbacks, too. Good equipment is expensive. It can all be destroyed during one unfortunate chase. Travel costs can be high. The chaser might have to travel many miles to reach a stormy area only to discover that the storms have died down. Competition is increasing. People with cell phones can catch terrific shots and allow television stations to use

Whether they're professionals or just enthusiasts, storm chasers often travel together.

them for free. Finally, storm seasons are unpredictable. In a fairly calm year, there is not much business for a storm chaser.

A small number of enthusiasts offer storm-chasing expeditions. These are tours where individuals or groups accompany chasers for the thrill or for the opportunity to photograph severe weather. The job of tour director has a number of disadvantages. The legal and insurance costs can be quite high. There is always the possibility that a tourist may be injured. And participants may not be willing to put up with trips that are canceled because of good weather.

The scientists who chase storms are usually professional meteorologists. Chasing is a small but extremely important part of what they do. During a tornado, they might try to place equipment in the storm's path. Well-placed sensors can record wind speeds, temperature, humidity, and **atmospheric pressure** within and outside the funnel. They might also test

Storm chasers use equipment to gather data.

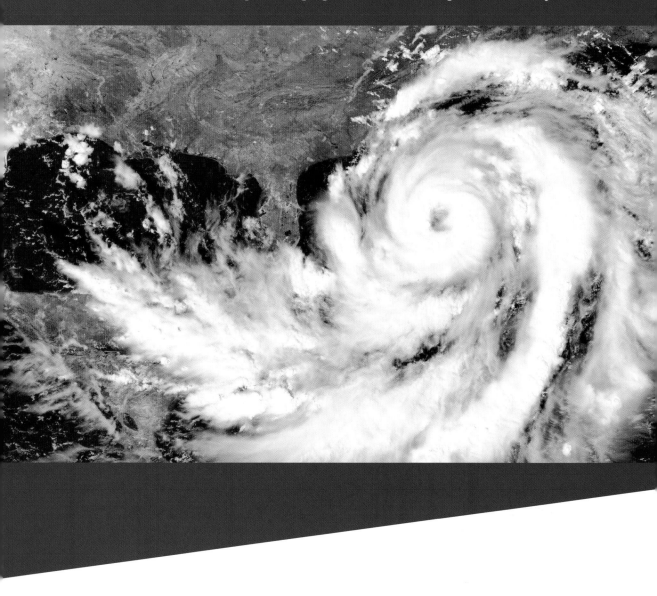

If meteorologists can see that a hurricane is going to hit land, they can tell people who live there to go somewhere safer.

new sensing equipment to see if it works well in tough conditions.

The data they gather will be analyzed later in the lab. It can help other meteorologists to better understand how storms form, grow, behave, and die out. This leads to better weather predictions and more accurate forecasts. Ultimately, the work of these scientists can save lives. They can understand a storm's mechanics as it is forming, so warnings can go out to the public. They can immediately report the extent of storm damage, so emergency teams can prepare appropriate responses.

THINK ABOUT ENGINEERING

There is always a need for better, faster, and more accurate instruments that measure conditions in the atmosphere. This is where engineers come in. Thanks to their work, we have weather satellites high above the earth. They transmit information such as temperatures and cloud movements on a large scale. Such data helps meteorologists to predict the weather.

CHAPTER 4

CURRENT ISSUES

At present, there are some exciting advancements in storm research. At the same time, **controversies** are arising about storm chasers themselves.

The National Severe Storms Laboratory (NSSL) in Norman, Oklahoma is conducting some of this groundbreaking research. Researchers at the NSSL study tornadoes, thunderstorms, wind, lightning, hail, floods, and winter weather. Their tornado researchers know that about 80 percent of tornadoes come out of rotating thunderstorms, or supercells. They are trying to learn why

Dr. Karen Kosiba is a severe weather expert. Here, in 2010, she works at the Doppler on Wheels, in New Cordell, Oklahoma.

some supercells produce tornadoes while others do not.

The Center for Severe Weather Research (CSWR), in Colorado, studies tornadoes and hurricanes. One of their most important tools is the Doppler on Wheels (DOW) network. It includes a number of vehicles equipped with instruments that measure wind speeds. Their DOWs have been used in storm research all over the world.

Lightning researchers have learned that shortly before a severe storm develops, lightning activity increases dramatically. They are finding better

*Even some of the most knowledgeable and experienced
storm chasers have been killed by tornadoes.*

ways to detect, record, and predict such "lightning jumps" and thus warn people more quickly of impending storms.

The scientists who do research are dedicated to working safely. But tornadoes can be unpredictable, and dangers always exist. In 2013, an enormous tornado killed three **veteran** chasers in Oklahoma. The same tornado picked up the car of a meteorologist for The Weather Channel and dropped it 200 yards (183 meters) away. These incidents involved experienced, skilled, safety-minded people.

Unfortunately, storm chasing also appeals to many thrill seekers. Rather than following storms to conduct research or gather data, they hope to feel the exhilaration of witnessing a tornado.

As meteorologists become more accurate in predicting stormy outbreaks, chasers are learning more quickly where they can find the storms. Sometimes, amateur storm chasers cause traffic jams and block

Storm chasers need to be aware of where the storm is heading, so they don't put themselves and others in danger.

roadways. Meteorologists in research vehicles cannot cut through all the traffic. Police, fire, and rescue vehicles are unable to reach damaged areas.

Reckless chasers do not take the dangers seriously. Some pose for photographs with a tornado approaching in the background. Others chase after tornadoes with children in the backseat of a vehicle.

Still others post their videos on the Internet, along with the audio. These chasers are heard squealing and laughing as objects are flung about by the high winds.

But those flying objects might have killed people, and the winds may have destroyed homes. Their indifference to the danger and destruction is especially **appalling** to those harmed by the storm.

Unfortunately, there are also some storm chasers who pretend to be scientists but are not. They invent fake research studies to explain why they are behaving so recklessly, and they try to make money by publicizing the "discoveries" that they make about storms.

THINK ABOUT ART

A few storm chasers are excellent photographers. They not only have quick reaction times to catch events as they happen, but they also are patient enough to wait for the perfect shot. Some prefer to show the human suffering caused by violent storms. Their work is important to the relief efforts that follow a disaster.

CHAPTER 5

CHASING YOUR INTEREST IN STORMS

If you are fascinated by dramatic weather, you might wish to become a storm spotter. Spotters take classes to learn how to report information to the NWS. Some work from their vehicles, but most stay at a fixed point. They report such things as large hail, downed power lines, uprooted trees, and heavy rainfall. They provide a real service to their communities by reporting conditions the NWS might not be aware of.

To become even more involved, you might consider a career in meteorology. You can prepare for such a career by obtaining a degree in meteorology or atmospheric sciences. With a bachelor's degree and some journalism experience, you might land a job as a broadcaster and perhaps report on storms as they are happening.

A master's or doctoral degree will involve more class time and some research. Your research may involve storm chasing for the purpose of taking measurements

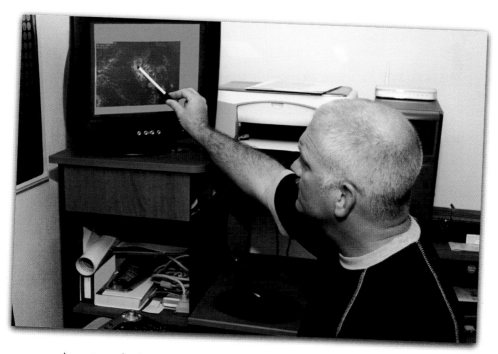

A meteorologist needs a strong background in science classes.

Storm chasers enjoy the thrill of extreme weather, but they know that this career can put their lives at risk.

or shooting videos. People who have completed advanced degrees often work with the NWS, teach at universities, do further research, or even work as airport meteorologists.

You should know that the NWS does not have job listings for storm chasers. And the NSSL states that chasing opportunities are rare and are only for specific data-collection projects. Those who do go out in the field during severe weather are usually research scientists or their students.

If you want to sell photos or videos of storms, you should ride with safe, experienced chasers for several years before going out on your own. You should also take classes to learn all you can about supercells, tornadoes, lightning, hurricanes, and storm safety. A degree is not required, but a cautious attitude is. Storm chasing can be exciting, breathtaking, and even inspiring. But safety should always be your first concern.

THINK ABOUT MATH

Many scientists in the field of meteorology have degrees in physics, math, and other sciences. Mathematicians and computer scientists are creating 3-D computer models of thunderstorms and tornadoes. They are using the models to learn why some thunderstorms become supercells and why some supercells produce tornadoes.

THINK ABOUT IT

Authorities are trying to figure out how to get the growing numbers of amateur storm chasers under control without impeding the work of legitimate chasers. Among other things, they have considered closing roads and issuing special permits to qualified chasers. How would you solve this problem?

Storm chasers have gathered important data about tornado wind speeds. How might such data be of value to architects and builders?

In the United States, there are more than 1,000 tornadoes every year—more than any other country in the world. Why do you think this country has such high numbers? What factors or conditions might cause so many tornadoes?

LEARN MORE

FURTHER READING

Challoner, Jack. *Hurricane & Tornado*. London: DK Publishing, 2014.

Jeffrey, Gary. *Hurricane Hunters and Tornado Chasers*. New York: Rosen Publishing Group, 2008.

Miller, Ron. *Chasing the Storm: Tornadoes, Meteorology, and Weather Watching*. Minneapolis: Twenty-First Century Books, 2014.

WEB SITES

Science with NOAA Research: Tornadoes
www.oar.noaa.gov/k12/html/tornadoes2.html
Find more information about tornadoes and tornado safety.

Surviving the Storm with Warren Faidley
www.stormchaser.com
Read about expert storm chaser Warren Faidley and his work.

Weather Wiz Kids: Tornadoes
www.weatherwizkids.com/weather-tornado.htm
Learn about tornadoes, supercells, waterspouts, dust devils, and more.

GLOSSARY

aftermath (AF-tur-math) the result of an event, especially a disastrous one

appalling (uh-PAW-ling) causing dismay or horror

atmospheric pressure (at-muhs-FEER-ik PREH-shur) the force exerted by the weight of the air at a given location; tornadoes develop in low-pressure conditions

controversies (KON-truh-vur-seez) prolonged public debates or arguments

enthusiasts (en-THOO-zee-ists) people filled with interest or passion for something

meteorologists (mee-tee-ur-AWL-uh-jists) scientists who study the atmosphere, including the climate and weather

phenomena (fuh-NAH-muh-nuh) facts or occurrences that can be observed

professional (pruh-FESH-uh-nuhl) someone in an occupation that requires special training or study

prone (PROHN) having a natural tendency toward something

stock photo agencies (STAHK FOH-toh AY-juhn-seez) companies that buy photographs so they can rent them to others

typhoons (tye-FOONZ) hurricanes that occur in the western Pacific Ocean

veteran (VET-ur-uhn) someone who has much experience in a particular field

videography (vid-ee-OG-ruh-fee) the art of shooting films or videos

vortex (VOR-tex) a whirling mass of air or water

INDEX

[21ST CENTURY SKILLS LIBRARY]